Gangs and Your Friends

TOOKIE SPEAKS OUT AGAINST GANG VIOLENCE™

Stanley "Tookie" Williams

with Barbara Cottman Becnel

The Rosen Publishing Group's
PowerKids Press™
New York

Published in 1996 by The Rosen Publishing Group, Inc.
29 East 21st Street, New York, NY 10010

First Edition

Photo credits: Cover by Michael Brandt; front cover inset, back cover and p. 4 © J. Patrick Forden; pp. 7, 8 by John Novajosky; pp. 11, 12 by Seth Dinnerman; p. 15 © Deborah Copaken/Gamma Liaison; p. 16 by Guillermina DeFerrari; p. 19 © Ray Solowinski/International Stock; p. 20 courtesy of the Williams family.

Williams, Stanley.
    Gangs and your friends / by Stanley "Tookie" Williams and Barbara Cottman Becnel.
      p.   cm. — (Tookie speaks out against gang violence)
    Includes index.
    Summary: A founder of the Crips in Los Angeles introduces kids to the way gangs operate focusing particularly on the powerful influence of "bad" friends.
    ISBN 0-8239-2341-X
    1. Gangs—United States—Juvenile literature. 2. Friendship—United States—Juvenile literature. 3. Crips (Gang)—Juvenile literature. [1. Gangs. 2. Friendship. 3. Crips (Gang).] I. Becnel, Barbara Cottman. II. Title. III. Series: Williams, Stanley. Tookie speaks out against gangs.
HV6789.W5 1996
364.1'06'6—dc20
                                            95-51328
                                              CIP
                                              AC

Manufactured in the United States of America

Contents

Big Took

Hello. My name is Stanley "Tookie" Williams. My mom calls me Tookie. So do most of my **homeboys** (HOME-boiz). Some homeboys call me Big Took because my muscles are very big from lifting weights. I started lifting weights as a teen in camp, after seeing older homeboys in my South Central Los Angeles neighborhood lift weights. These homeboys were big and strong. They liked to fight. Many people were afraid of them. The older homeboys got to boss everyone around. I wanted to be like them.

◀ *Tookie didn't want to be bossed around by bigger kids in the neighborhood. He decided to lift weights to get stronger.*

The Crips

When I was 17, I met Raymond Washington. He had big muscles too. We became friends. The two of us created a gang called the Crips. After that, Raymond and I started telling lots of homeboys what to do. And they did it.

When Raymond and I gave orders to our homeboys, they got into trouble. We got into plenty of trouble too. But we thought we were being "**down**" (DOWN), being really cool homeboys.

Many gang members think that ▶
having big muscles is cool.

Homeboys

"Homeboy" is a slang word that means friend.

But a homeboy is not a true friend if he tries to make you do bad things—like join a gang and sell drugs, or steal, or carry a gun, or even kill someone. A homeboy is not a true friend if he calls you chicken or a coward or a punk when you don't do what he says.

◀ *Sometimes people try to get kids to do bad things, such as selling drugs.*

9

True Friendship

A true friend is someone who really cares about you.

If you are about to get into a fight, a true friend will try to stop you from fighting. If you are about to join a gang, a true friend will try to talk you out of it. A true friend doesn't want you to be hurt. A true friend doesn't ever want you to hurt somebody else just to prove you're down, or tough, or cool.

A true friend will try to protect you from harm, not lead you to it. ▶

Friendship and Power

We spend a lot of time with our friends. We tell our secrets to friends. We share our lunch money and candy and clothes with friends. We count on our friends to make us feel better when we're afraid or angry or sad.

We really **trust** (TRUST) our friends. We listen to them. We worry about what they think of us. We want them to like us. For all these reasons, we give our friends a lot of power over us. That is why it's important for you to pick true friends to hang out with.

◄ *Friends have the power to help or hurt one another. A true friend is one who helps you.*

The Word "Gang"

Nowadays, some people use the word gang for any big group of kids who hang around together. But there is nothing wrong with having lots of friends. Having many true friends to play with and be with does *not* mean you are part of a gang.

A real gang is any group of grown-ups, teenagers, or kids your age that go around punching or shooting people. Gangs do other bad things like deal drugs, steal cars, and rob stores.

Gangs are usually made up of people who hurt others. ▶

Trust Yourself

When I was a boy, there were times when I knew that something I was going to do was bad. Just before I did it, my stomach felt strange. A voice inside my head said, "Don't." But I would do it anyway. My home-boys and I got into a lot of trouble with the police.

You can learn from my mistakes. Trust yourself. Most of the time you will do the right thing and you won't get into trouble.

◀ *Trust the voice inside your head when it tells you to stay away from danger.*

Following Rules

My sister and I went to speech class because my mother wanted us to speak clearly and use proper English. But my homeboys used curse words to sound cool. That was the rule, and I followed it. I didn't want my homeboys to make fun of me.

What I did was dumb. You need to speak well to do well in school and to get a good job as an adult. It hurt me to follow my homeboys' rules.

You need to learn skills such as math and English to be successful. ▶

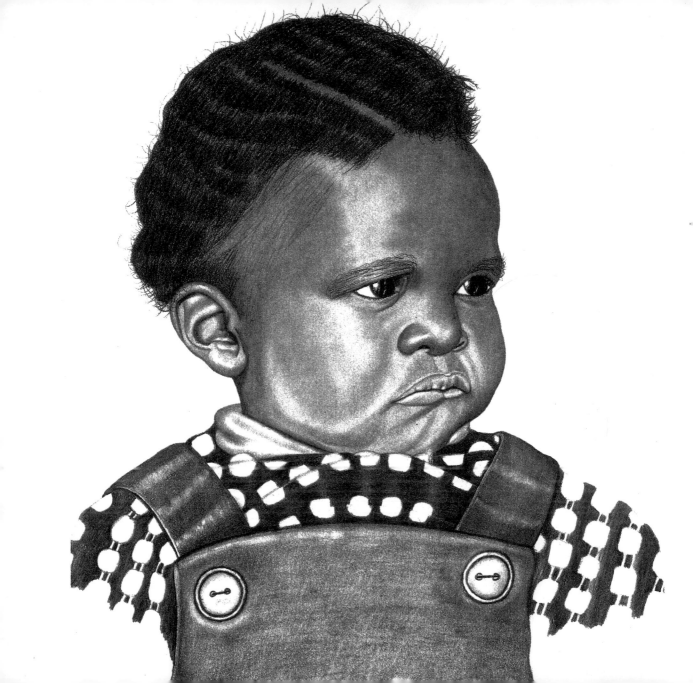

Breaking Away from Gangs

If you are not in a gang, be smart—don't join one. If you are a gang member, ask yourself: "Am I scared when I do what my homeboys want? Do I do things even when I know they are wrong?" Tell the truth. You're the only one listening.

I think you'll answer yes to both questions. But I believe in you. Your next step can be to leave the gang, to stop spending time with your homeboys. Then find yourself some new friends, true friends who really care about you.

◀ *Tookie believed in himself. He learned that he can draw well. He drew this picture of himself as a baby.*

Be Yourself, Love Yourself

It feels good to break free from gang life, to know that you don't need to do bad things to prove to your homeboys that you're cool. These days, I am the only person I need to prove anything to.

It's much easier just being myself. I even found out I have a hidden **talent** (TAL-ent). I can draw really well.

You can do the same thing—and more. So be yourself and love yourself. No homeboy in a gang can do that for you.

Glossary

to be **down** (DOWN) To be ready to do
anything, no matter how dangerous or how
bad, because your homeboys expect it of
you.

homeboy (HOME-boi) A slang word that means
friend or partner.

talent (TAL-ent) Ability to do something really well.

trust (TRUST) To depend on; to believe in.

Index